# CONSERVING THE ATMOSPHERE

John Baines

STECK-VAUGHN
LIBRARY
A Division of Steck-Vaughn Company

# Conserving Our World

**Acid Rain**
**Conserving Rain Forests**
**Waste and Recycling**
**Conserving the Atmosphere**
**Protecting Wildlife**
**The Spread of Deserts**

**Cover**: The atmosphere surrounds the Earth, protecting it and supporting all life forms.

**Series editor**: Sue Hadden
**Series designer**: Ross George

**Published in the United States in 1990 by Steck-Vaughn Co., Austin, Texas**, a subsidiary of National Education Corporation.

© Copyright 1989 Wayland (Publishers) Ltd.

First published in 1989 by Wayland (Publishers) Ltd.

**Library of Congress Cataloging-in-Publication Data**

Baines, John D.
 Conserving the atmosphere/John Baines.
  p. cm. — (Conserving our world)
 Includes bibliographical references.
 Summary: An introduction to the problems confronting the Earth's atmosphere, fossil fuels and their effects, the effect of chemicals on the ozone layer, radioactivity, and other forms of pollution and what can be done to stop the destruction of the atmosphere.
 ISBN 0-8114-3451-6 Softcover Binding
 ISBN 0-8114-2388-3 Hardcover Library Binding
 1. Air—Pollution—Juvenile literature. 2. Air quality management—Juvenile literature. [1. Air—Pollution.
2. Atmosphere.] I. Title. II. Series
TD883.13.B35 1989       89-22042
363.73'92—dc20         CIP
               AC

Typeset by Multifacit Graphics, Keyport, NJ
Printed in the United States.
Bound in the United States by Lake Book, Melrose Park, IL

  4 5 6 7 8 9 0 LB 94 93 92

# Contents

What scientists, weather forecasters, airplane pilots, and other experts call the "atmosphere," most people know as the "air." Neither of these two words adequately describes what the air is or what it does. Even a scientific description gives us only a partial understanding of what the atmosphere means to us.

The atmosphere plays a large part in our daily lives, but most of the time we do not stop to think about it. We notice brilliant sunshine, pouring rain, strong winds, or snow, but we rarely pause to think about the atmospheric conditions that cause them.

Authors and poets use descriptions of the atmosphere to match the mood of their literature.

***People can make use of the atmosphere for sports, such as hang gliding.***

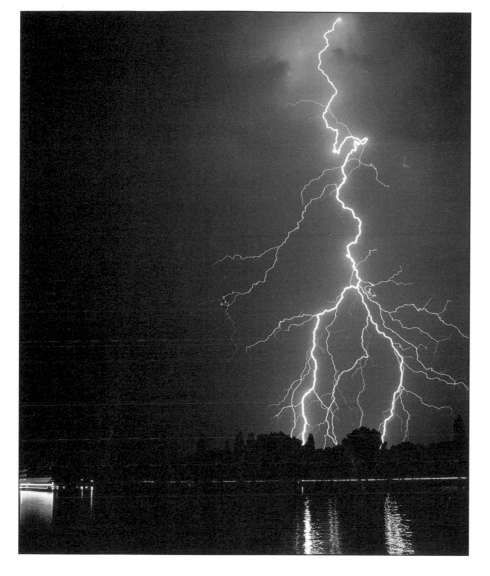

*When an electrical charge forks from a storm cloud down to earth, it creates some spectacular effects, which we call lightning.*

It may be "the stillness of the night air," "the raging of a storm," or "the enchantment of a sunset." Film producers use storms, winds, thunder, and lightning to add extra drama to a particularly tense or frightening scene. Painters and photographers of landscapes use dramatic skies to set a mood for their pictures. We even use the word atmosphere to describe the feelings we have about a place. A school that is enjoyed by its pupils is said to have a happy atmosphere.

The air around us is more than just a mixture of gases, water, and dirt. It provides the oxygen necessary for us to survive, although we usually do not even notice we are breathing. If we have a headache or need to think about a problem, a walk in the fresh air can make us feel much better. Of course, the atmosphere does not just support us—it gives life to all the plants and animals that share the earth with us. Therefore, it is very precious and we should learn to value it.

In this book we shall take a close look at what the atmosphere is and how it supports life on earth. We will also think about how our activities are changing the atmosphere and the dangers that arise from this. Finally, we will examine what is being done, and what still needs to be done, to ensure that the atmosphere remains in good condition for the future.

# What Does the Atmosphere Do?

The atmosphere is made up of a mixture of gases, water vapor, dust, and dirt. It surrounds and protects the earth from bombardment by meteorites and harmful radiation. It supports life. Without it, the earth would be as barren as the moon. There would be no oceans, rivers, lakes, plants, animals, or you.

*This alpine meadow is full of flowers, thanks to the atmosphere surrounding our planet.*

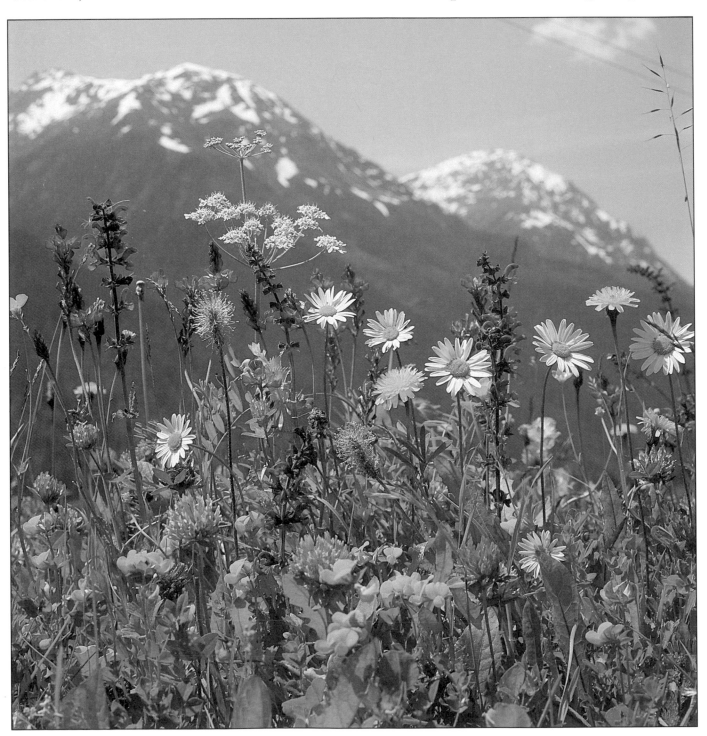

*The gases that make up the atmosphere are invisible, but water vapor can be seen where it has made clouds. This picture, taken from far above the earth, shows the continents of Africa and Antarctica very clearly.*

*The diagram below shows the different gas layers that make up the earth's atmosphere.*

## The Layers of the Earth's Atmosphere

**Exosphere**  about 300 miles
Outermost layer of earth's atmosphere.

**Ionosphere**  about 40 miles
Layer with very high temperatures. Electrically charged particles called ions move freely around.

**Stratosphere**  about 25 miles
Cloud-free layer at a constant temperature.

**Tropopause** (boundary of Troposphere)

**Troposphere**
This varies daily from a maximum of about 11 miles over the equator to about 3.7 miles at the poles.
All our weather conditions occur within this zone.

Height above sea level (in miles)

0

## Nitrogen and oxygen

In the lower atmosphere where we live, the essential gases are nitrogen (almost 79 percent), oxygen (almost 21 percent), and trace gases including carbon dioxide, argon, neon, ozone, and krypton (all together less than one percent). Within that one percent are now a number of new human-made gases, some of which are highly poisonous, such as dioxin.

The amount of each gas is very important. If the level of oxygen dropped significantly, then animals would not be able to breathe. If it was much higher, the whole planet would be in danger of catching on fire. Even the miniscule amounts of trace gases are very important. Each one plays a vital part in protecting life on earth.

## Water vapor

The atmosphere absorbs energy from the sun and from the surface of the earth. Where the air is warmest, it rises. Cool air comes in to take its place, creating winds. The air absorbs moisture from the ocean, rivers, lakes, vegetation, and the soil. This becomes water vapor in the air and can be carried hundreds of miles in the wind before returning to earth as rain or snow. These movements are so regular that it is possible to divide the world into climatic zones.

## The balance of nature

The ingredients of the atmosphere have been held in balance for millions of years, but pollution by human activity is upsetting this balance and creating many problems. The atmosphere is getting too warm, the protective ozone layer is being destroyed, acid rain is damaging lakes and forests, and dangerous chemicals are poisoning people, plants, and animals.

Conserving the atmosphere has become a major concern, not only for conservationists, but also for politicians, industrialists, farmers, and the international community as a whole.

*Winds are the movement of the atmosphere. They follow regular patterns, as shown in the map. The names reflect their importance to the early trading ships.*

**World Winds**

Equator

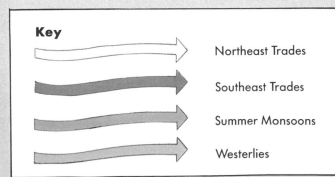

**Key**

Northeast Trades

Southeast Trades

Summer Monsoons

Westerlies

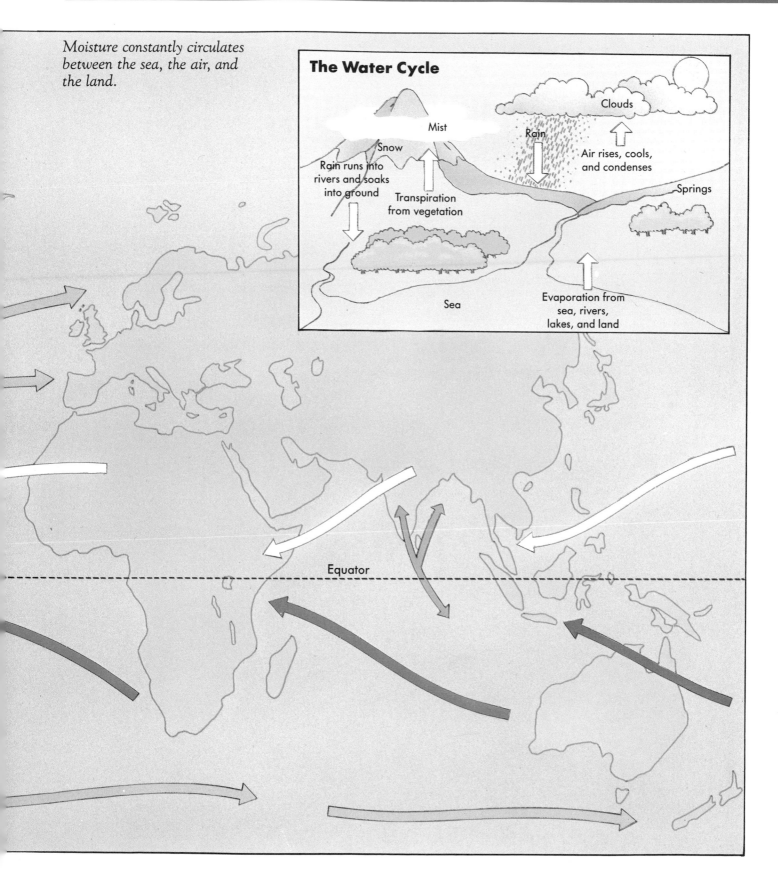

Moisture constantly circulates between the sea, the air, and the land.

**The Water Cycle**

Mist

Snow

Clouds

Rain

Air rises, cools, and condenses

Rain runs into rivers and soaks into ground

Transpiration from vegetation

Springs

Sea

Evaporation from sea, rivers, lakes, and land

Equator

# Fossil Fuels and the Atmosphere

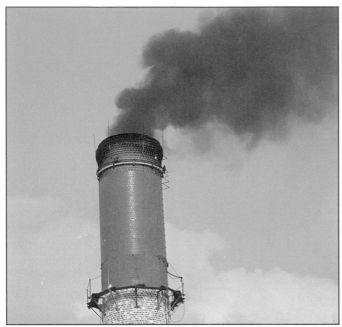

Thirty years ago few people thought pollution could become a problem that would affect the whole planet. We now know that pollution is damaging the earth's climatic and ecological systems. One of the major causes of pollution is the burning of fossil fuels such as oil, coal, and natural gas. These fuels are used to generate electricity, to make metals out of ores, to make chemicals, to heat homes, offices, and factories, and to power vehicles. When the fuels are burned the waste products are released through chimneys or exhaust pipes, polluting the air.

*Fossil fuels like coal produce smoke which can pollute the atmosphere (left). However, much of what looks like pollution is water vapor from cooling towers (below).*

10

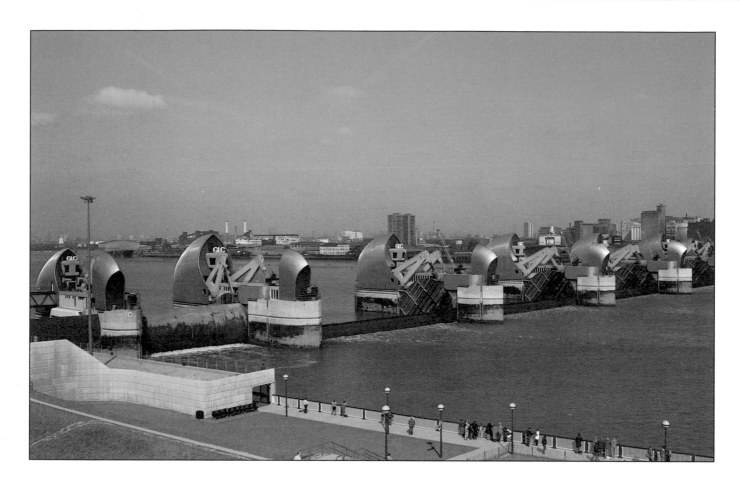

*In the 1950s, storms and high tides coincided to flood low-lying areas of southeast England. In the 1980s a barrage was built across the Thames River to protect London from flooding.*

## Global warming

The temperature of the earth today is at its highest recorded level. Since 1900 it has risen by 0.9°F, and a rise of another 2.7°F is inevitable in the next fifty years. This may not seem much, and some people might even think it is a trend to be encouraged. However, since the last ice age, some 10,000 years ago, the world's temperature has risen by only 7.2°F.

No one can predict the precise effect of such a rapid warming, but it is a question that world scientists have addressed. Their alarming predictions are as follows.

## A rise in sea level

During the earth's history there have been many changes in the sea level. It was much lower during the ice ages when more water was held frozen in glaciers and ice sheets. Today, higher temperatures are causing more of the ice to melt and the sea level is rising. Since 1900, the level has risen by 4 to 6 inches, and by the middle of the next century it could rise by an additional three feet or more. This is sufficient to put large areas of coastal or tidal cities such as New York and London at risk of regular flooding, and also to flood much of the best low-lying agricultural areas. In Bangladesh where the Ganges River reaches the sea, 15 million people could lose their homes. In prosperous Western countries, there is money available to improve defenses against the oceans, but developing countries are likely to suffer more frequent flooding.

HURRICANE GILBERT
SEPT. 15 1988
9 AM EDT

*This photograph from a satellite shows Hurricane Gilbert which caused terrible damage in the Caribbean in 1988.*

*Opposite Global warming may cause more floods in cities at sea level, like Calcutta.*

## More extreme weather patterns

Over the last twenty years, the weather over the world has become more extreme and many scientists attribute this to global warming. In Great Britain in 1987 and 1988 there were two storms in which the strongest winds for 250 years were recorded. Hurricanes in the Caribbean and the South Pacific are becoming more destructive and there have been devastating droughts in Africa, Australia, and the United States. Such events do occur naturally from time to time, but freak conditions are causing them more and more often.

## The major climatic zones will move

This will be most noticeable outside the tropics and will affect some of the most fertile and productive agricultural areas. Was the serious drought in the Midwest in 1988 an isolated occurrence, or was it a sign of things to come? Agriculture in other countries, including Canada and the Soviet Union, will probably benefit.

Strong winds are extremely powerful. In October 1987, record high winds blew down over half a million trees in southern Great Britain and caused great damage to houses and cars (left). In 1988, Hurricane Gilbert caused chaos in Jamaica, even throwing airplanes around (below).

You have just read that global warming may cause the oceans to rise, more extreme weather patterns, and a shift of climatic zones. Predictions are not always reliable, but there is agreement that the earth is warming and that this will affect the climate. This in itself is a problem. For example, major developments using water, such as hydroelectric power stations and irrigation systems, rely upon accurate predictions of the climate. These are based on climatic statistics from the past. In 1985, an international

*The Midwest, one of the world's major cereal-producing areas, suffered a catastrophic drought in 1988. This corn has hardly grown, although with normal rainfall it would be three feet high. Many American farmers suffered great losses from this drought.*

conference in Austria concluded that such climatic data was no longer a reliable guide. What do the planners use now to help them design new systems?

## The "greenhouse" effect

Some of the gases in the atmosphere are known as "greenhouse" gases. The heat of the sun can penetrate the gases, but its escape is slowed down. Without these gases, the world would be about 72°F cooler—too cold for life. If the gases increase, then not enought heat would be able to escape, and the world would become too hot to inhabit.

**The diagram** below **shows how carbon is released into the atmosphere.**

Although about thirty "greenhouse" gases are known, 40 percent of the global warming is caused by one gas—carbon dioxide. It is one of the gases formed when fossil fuels are burned. The amounts found in the atmosphere are very

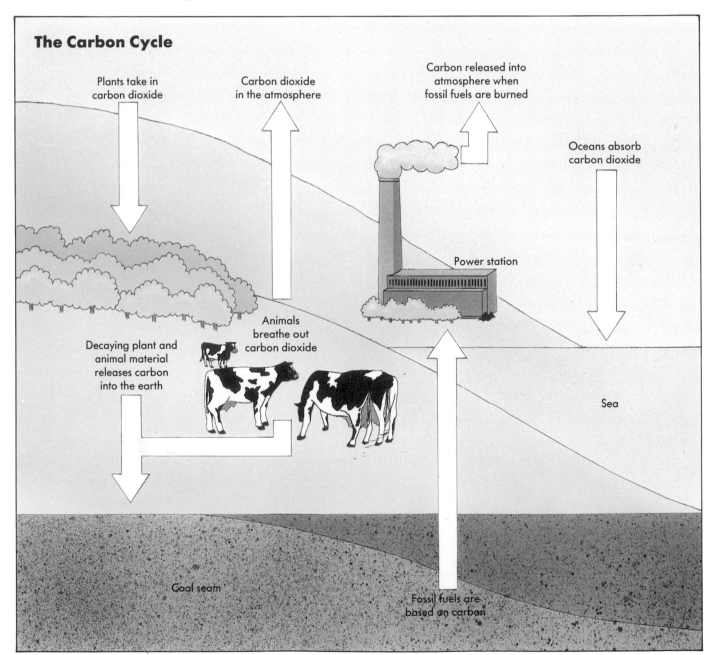

**The Carbon Cycle**

Plants take in carbon dioxide

Carbon dioxide in the atmosphere

Carbon released into atmosphere when fossil fuels are burned

Oceans absorb carbon dioxide

Power station

Decaying plant and animal material releases carbon into the earth

Animals breathe out carbon dioxide

Sea

Coal seam

Fossil fuels are based on carbon

## How the "Greenhouse" Effect Works

Gases that make up the "Greenhouse" roof

| Exhaust fumes | Oil | Coal |
| --- | --- | --- |

| Other gases | Carbon dioxide | |
| --- | --- | --- |
| Vegetation | Cattle | Fertilizers |
| Methane | | Nitrogen |

| Aerosol sprays | Hamburger cartons | Refrigerators |
| --- | --- | --- |
| CFC gases | | |

Incoming solar radiation

Some heat radiation escapes but gases trap the rest like glass in a greenhouse

Greenhouse roof

small, but are rising dangerously fast. In 1850, for every million gallons of air, there were 280 gallons of carbon dioxide (usually expressed as 280 parts per million). By 1958 the level had risen to 333 parts per million and in 1988 the figure had reached 370. As the levels rise, the "greenhouse" effect worsens. As the temperature rises, more water evaporates and becomes water vapor in the atmosphere. The water vapor is even more effective than carbon dioxide in preventing the earth's heat from escaping. The effects of this

*The diagram* above *illustrates how the "greenhouse" effect works. Cutting down our use of fossil fuels and saving the world's forests can stop the problem from getting worse.*

are not felt immediately because it takes many years for the land, oceans, and atmosphere to heat up. However, most scientists consider that a further rise in temperature of 2.7°F is inevitable over the next fifty years.

Left *It is hard to imagine that even grazing cattle can contribute to the "greenhouse" effect, but cows are known to produce much methane.*

*The diagram* below *predicts the effect of various greenhouse gases on global warming.*

Another "greenhouse" gas that is causing concern is methane. The amount in the atmosphere is increasing at the rate of one to two percent per year. It comes mainly from rotting vegetation in swamps and paddy fields, and from the mining and distribution of fossil fuels. Cattle also release methane when they are ruminating. In addition, methane slows down the rate at which the atmosphere can clean itself of other pollutants, such as sulfur dioxide. This is a major cause of acid rain.

## Acid rain

Acid rain is causing great damage to lakes, rivers, and forests in many parts of the world, especially the United States, Canada, Scandinavia, and the mainland of Europe.

Sulfur dioxide and nitrogen oxides, formed when fossil fuels are burned, are two of the main culprits. Water vapor in the atmosphere absorbs these chemicals and becomes a weak solution of sulfuric and nitric acids. This eventually reaches the ground as rain, snow, or mist, and is thus known as acid rain. Throughout Great Britain the rainfall is ten times more acidic than is normal.

Some rain is so polluted that it is 1,000 times more acidic than normal.

The atmosphere is never still, as air moves vertically and horizontally. Pollution is carried in the air, sometimes for a week or more before it finally returns to earth. The damage it eventually causes may therefore occur a long way from the original source of the pollution.

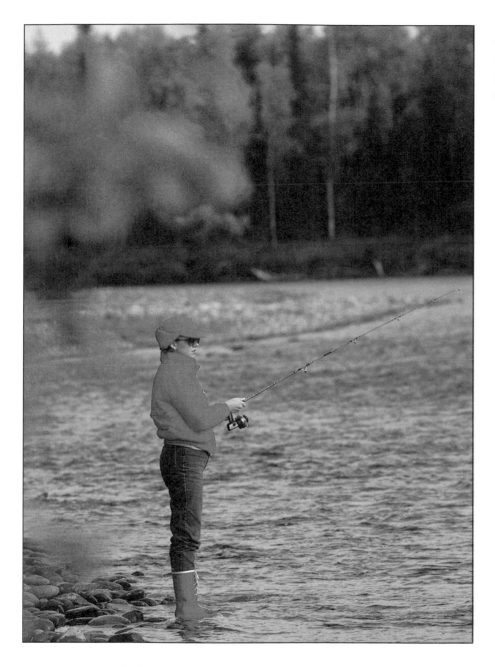

*Fishing is a popular pastime but it may be threatened, as many fish are becoming casualties of acid rain.*

## Damage to lakes and trees

One of the worst-affected areas in Europe is Scandinavia. The pollution is carried there from the major industrial areas of Great Britain, Eastern Europe, and West Germany. Norway receives about 220,000 tons of sulfur in the air from other European countries every year. Canada claims that 50 percent of the sulfur dioxide it receives comes from the United States. The first sign of the problem in Norway was that many lakes were losing their fish. Some seemed to have none at all. When this was investigated, it was noted that all the lakes had high acid levels. For a lake to remain healthy, it needs a pH of around 6.5. In some of the cases investigated, the pH had dropped to 4.5; a level at which the lakes could not support life at all. The main culprit was found to be sulfur dioxide, carried by the wind into Norway from other countries.

It was not until the 1960s that it was noticed that acid rain was also damaging trees and forests. Coniferous trees are the worst affected. The tops of the trees are the first to suffer, as they lose the needles that use the sunlight to grow. Where the pollution is more severe, needles are also lost lower down on the tree. Eventually the tree becomes so weak that it is attacked by insects and fungi and dies. In the hills of Czechoslovakia, the damage is so severe that whole areas once forested are now treeless moorland. Damage to coniferous and deciduous trees has now been found in areas not thought to be at risk.

## Other damage

Many buildings in or near industrial areas are showing the effects of acid rain. The stone decorations on some historic buildings have been dissolved by acid rain so much that they are unrecognizable.

People are also at risk if they eat certain foods. Fish from acid lakes sometimes contain poisonous metals that have been dissolved out of the soil. The livers of moose, a delicacy in Scandinavia, are also often contaminated with these metals.

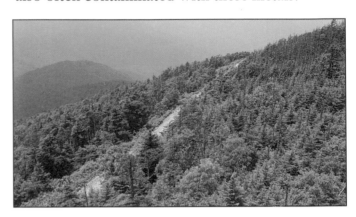

**Above** *These dying trees in North Carolina are showing the effects of acid rain.*

**Below** *The stonework of the remains of the Parthenon in Athens is deteriorating very rapidly because of acid rain.*

## Vehicles and the atmosphere

There are about 550 million vehicles in the world today, enough to make a line of traffic long enough to stretch around the world about forty times. Of all the forms of transportation, cars and trucks cause the most pollution. We have already seen that vehicle exhaust fumes contribute both to acid rain and to the build-up of carbon dioxide in the atmosphere.

Gasoline engines pump a number of harmful gases into the air. Carbon monoxide interferes with the supply of oxygen to the brain and can

*Gasoline engines pump a lot of harmful gases into the atmosphere at street level, where they are inhaled by people. Leaded gas is especially harmful to children.*

lead to dizziness and headaches. Hydrocarbons (unburned fuel) and nitrogen oxides react with sunlight to form ozone, which collects near the ground in traffic smogs. Such smogs are widespread in the United States and Europe. They can irritate the eyes and lungs, damage crops, and corrode many materials. The United States blames 3,000 deaths a year on air pollution.

In many countries, gasoline also contains lead, which ends up in the atmosphere. It is poisonous and can cause brain damage or behavioral problems in young children.

Diesel engines power most large vehicles like buses and trucks. They are also becoming more popular in cars. They use less fuel, but if they are not tuned properly, they can create a lot of black smoke and soot. It is suspected that this can cause cancer in some people.

The pollution from exhausts is particularly bad in towns and cities, where vehicles are jammed together in great numbers on tightly packed networks of roads, hemmed in by buildings.

*Of all forms of transportation, vehicles cause the most pollution. Traffic jams, like this one in Bangkok, occur everywhere.*

Along the streets the air can be very unpleasant to breathe and, along the busiest ones, it is positively harmful. The effects of pollution spread far from the towns and the highways carrying vehicles between them. In Switzerland, for example, the forests that protect villages and popular ski slopes from avalanches of snow are being killed by traffic fumes.

Vehicles have a bad environmental record. None of the pollution they cause is necessary.

## Cleaning up fossil fuels

There is only one real solution to the pollution caused by fossil fuels: clean up the atmosphere. Although we can filter pollution out of the air we breathe inside buildings, outside the only way is to stop the pollution from getting into the air in the first place. We have the technology to do this, but it is expensive and some say the costs are greater than the benefits. Pollution caused by burning fossil fuels can be reduced in a number of ways:

## Using less fuel

Our way of life in the industrialized world is dependent upon using vast quantities of energy.

Fossil fuels are responsible for producing most of the energy we need.

We are learning to use fuel more efficiently, but a lot is still wasted. Heat escapes from badly insulated buildings, power stations discharge warm cooling water into rivers and the ocean instead of reusing it, trucks return empty after delivering their loads, and many of us are reluctant to leave our cars at home and use public transportation instead. It has been estimated that we could use 50 percent less fuel and still enjoy the same standard of living we do today, if more energy conservation measures were introduced.

*The diagram below shows that public transportation is an efficient means of travel. It is also better for the environment.*

### Vehicles and Atmosphere

| | | Number of miles per person |
|---|---|---|
| | A small car can carry one person for 22.4 miles on 1 gallon of fuel | 22.4 |
| | 4 people in a small car | 89.6 |
| | A bus with 40 passengers carries each person the equivalent of 124 miles on 1 gallon of fuel | 124 |
| | A train carries each person the equivalent of 136 miles on 1 gallon of fuel | 136 |

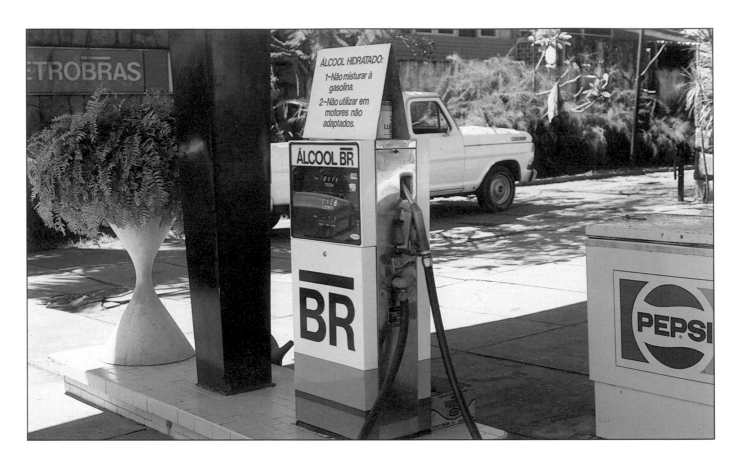

## Using less polluting fuels

Some fuels cause less pollution than gasoline or diesel oil. Brazil has to import most of its oil and so, to save money, alcohol is being used instead of gasoline. It is made from sugar cane and cassava. The exhaust fumes are almost clean enough to breathe. Brazil has also experimented with the use of vegetable oils to power diesel engines. These also cause much less pollution.

The atmosphere itself contains abundant energy. The wind is used to drive ships and windmills. Experiments are now taking place to use windmills to generate electricity. Waves are formed by the wind and they too can be used to generate electricity. Photoelectric cells use the energy directly from the sun to make electricity. Nuclear power is often proposed as a clean replacement for fossil fuels, but there is a great deal of opposition to it because it is potentially so dangerous.

*In Brazil, cars are fueled by alcohol made from farm crops such as sugar cane and cassava. This nonpolluting fuel is obtained from a pump, just like gas.*

## Cleaning up the pollution at its source

It is possible to prevent pollution from entering the atmosphere. The smoke from power stations can have its sulfur dioxide content removed before it reaches the atmosphere. Cars can be equipped with catalytic converters so that the harmful carbon monoxide, nitrogen oxides, and hydrocarbons are converted into less harmful carbon dioxide and water. But there is a cost. Our electric bill could go up by as much as 10 percent, and the cost of a car by between 3 and 5 percent. This is not a very high price to pay for a clean and healthy environment, and it is certainly cheaper and better than damaged forests, crumbling buildings, and poor health.

## Stop the destruction of rain forests

Forests take in carbon dioxide and help control the amount of carbon dioxide in the atmosphere, reducing the ''greenhouse'' effect. The huge areas of tropical forests in South America, Africa, and Southeast Asia are particularly important, but they are being removed very rapidly. As well as trying to reduce the amount of forest that is chopped down, we need to plant more forests. Gregg Marland of the Tennessee Institute for Energy estimates that to clean the atmosphere of the 5.5 billion tons of carbon dioxide created each year by burning fossil fuels, 1.7 billion acres (an area 14 times the size of France) of new forests are needed.

**Above** *The huge tropical rain forests of the world are disappearing rapidly.*

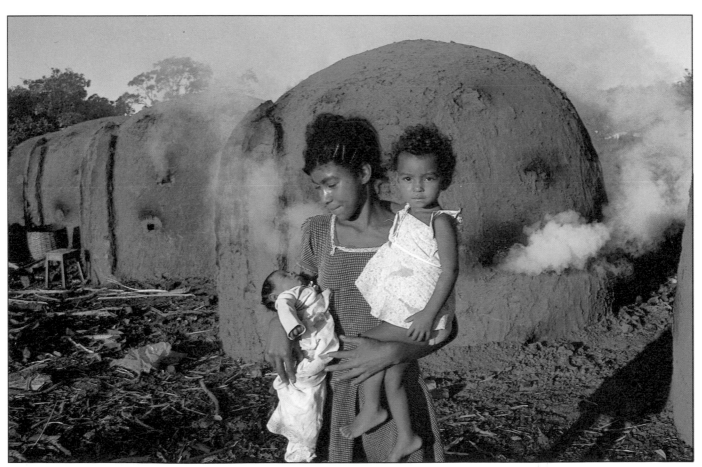

*Much of the cleared wood from tropical rain forests is burned to form charcoal. The burning adds to the amount of carbon dioxide in the atmosphere.*

## International cooperation

A lot is being done to reduce the pollution caused by burning fossil fuels, but it is still not enough. Research in Scandinavia shows that we will have to reduce the amount of sulfur dioxide and nitrogen oxides in the atmosphere by 80 percent to ensure a healthy environment.

Over the last ten years Europe has reduced the amount of sulfur dioxide pumped into the atmosphere by 25 percent. During the next ten years it will be reduced by a further 30 percent, thanks to more efficient use of fossil fuels and pollution control. Countries are showing that they are willing to cooperate with each other to solve the problem. In 1979, thirty countries signed an agreement to reduce their emissions of sulfur dioxide. In 1985 they fixed a reduction of

*Pollution of the atmosphere is an international problem. Members of the United Nations regularly meet to reach solutions.*

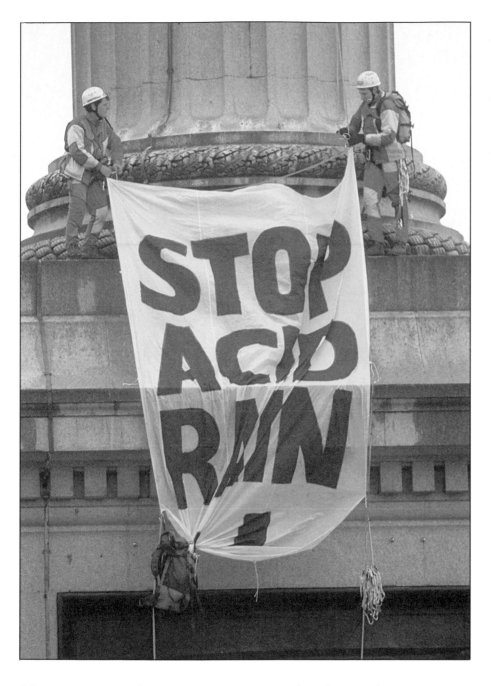

*An important step toward cleaning up the atmosphere is to raise public awareness of pollution. Here two Greenpeace campaigners display a banner in central London.*

30 percent as their goal, creating what has become known as the "30 Percent Club." There are now attempts to get similar agreements for nitrogen oxides, but nothing so far to reduce the amount of carbon dioxide.

To understand the scale of the problem and the solutions needed, more information is required. In 1980 the United Nations set up the Global Environmental Monitoring System which now has 175 sites in forty-two countries monitoring the state of the atmosphere. All the data are collected centrally from the participants to enable a global picture to be drawn.

The United Nations also runs an education program. This aims to tell people about the state of the environment, what needs to be done to protect it, and what is being done by nations individually and in cooperation with each other.

## Clean Exhausts Are Possible

The pollution from vehicles in cities such as Los Angeles and Tokyo became so severe that people decided they would no longer tolerate it. Very strict laws now make it illegal for any vehicle to exceed certain levels of pollution. The laws are so strict that one European car, on average, puts out as much nitrogen oxide as twelve vehicles in California.

The most successful way of reducing pollution from gasoline-engined cars is to add a catalytic converter. This is a small device fitted into the exhaust system of the car. It converts 90 percent of the harmful hydrocarbons, nitrogen oxides, and carbon monoxide into less harmful carbon dioxide, nitrogen, and water. It will work effectively only if unleaded gasoline is used. As a result unleaded gasoline is most popular where the exhaust emission controls are strictest and cars are inspected regularly.

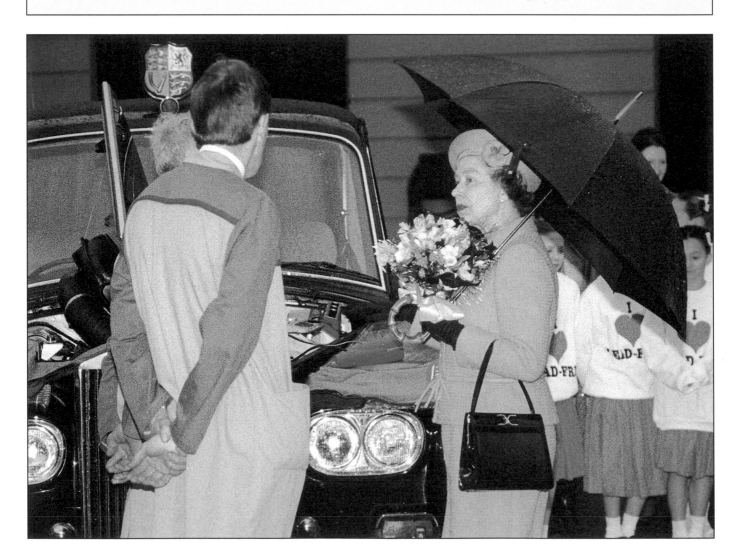

*In February 1989, Queen Elizabeth II delighted British environmentalists by announcing that her fleet of cars would all be converted to run on unleaded gas.*

## Lead in Gasoline

Lead is added to gasoline to improve an engine's performance. But lead is poisonous and highly dangerous for young children as it can damage the development of the brain. It can also cause them to be abnormally active and aggressive.

There is now a move in most countries to reduce or remove lead in gasoline. For example, in Great Britain the amount of lead in gasoline has been reduced from .056 to .021 ounces per gallon. As a result, the amount of lead in the air over the whole country has reduced from 8,000 to 3,200 tons. In West Germany, the use of lead in gasoline was banned in 1988.

Most cars will run on lead-free gasoline without any modification to the engine. Most others require only a cheap modification. Despite lead-free gasoline being cheaper in Great Britain than normal gasoline, only one driver in a thousand was using it at the start of 1988.

The benefits of using lead-free gasoline are:

• Less pollution, especially if cars are also fitted with a catalytic converter.

• Lower fuel bills. With lead-free gasoline the cars usually use less fuel.

• Engines, exhausts, and engine oil last longer, reducing the cost of regular maintenance.

*As unleaded gas becomes more widely available, more motorists are using it.*

## How to Reduce Exhaust Pollution

• Better technology. Scientists have developed "lean burn" engines. These use more oxygen so that the fuel is burned completely and causes less pollution.

• Regular maintenance. A well-tuned engine produces less pollution.

• Driving smoothly. Rapid acceleration uses a lot of fuel and increases pollution.

• Driving more slowly. A car traveling at 87 miles per hour produces twice the nitrogen oxides per mile as one traveling at 43 miles per hour.

• Checking tire pressures. Soft tires create more resistance and therefore more gasoline is used, but it is dangerous to pump in too much air.

• Whenever possible use public transportation, bicycle, or walk. The last two are pollution free and are healthy.

## The ozone layer

Ozone is a form of oxygen that is found in very small quantities in the upper atmosphere. Between 10 and 13 miles above the surface of the earth it is concentrated in a narrow layer less than a few miles thick. This layer is very important to life on earth because it filters out 99 percent of the sun's ultraviolet radiation, which would otherwise damage plants and animals.

The importance of this ozone layer has been known for a long time. Since the 1950s it has been monitored by the British Antarctic Survey in Antarctica. Little attention was paid to this data until the 1980s when it was discovered that, year after year, the amount of ozone in the upper atmosphere over Antarctica was getting less and less. In fact, during the winter of 1987, a huge hole as large as the United States developed in the ozone layer. The findings were confirmed by a weather satellite that had also been monitoring

*This photograph, taken in 1986 from the satellite NIMBUS-7, shows the extent of the ozone hole over Antarctica. The hole is shown by the areas of gray and mauve. During the winter of 1988, it was reported that the hole extended as far as South Island, New Zealand.*

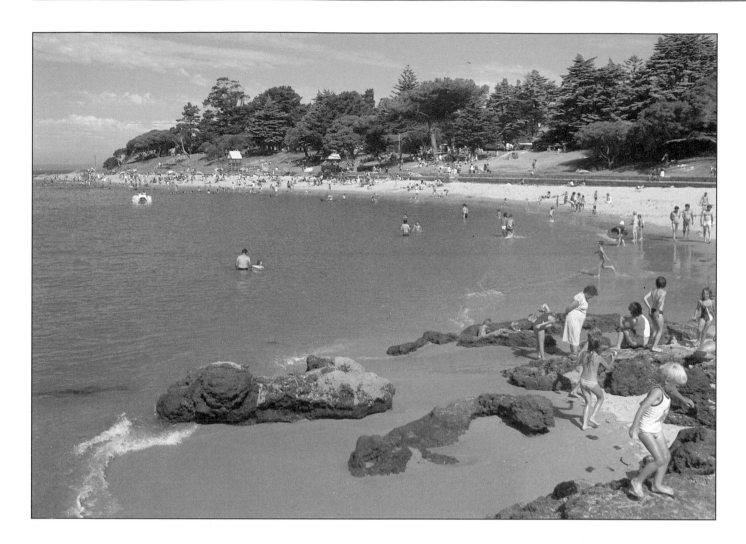

*The ozone layer protects us from the sun's harmful ultraviolet radiation. If it is damaged, the risk of skin cancer for some sunbathers like these on Philips Island beach, Australia, may increase.*

the ozone layer for years, but because no one believed it was important, the computer analyzing the data had been programmed to ignore it. By chance, the world had discovered the beginnings of an environmental disaster.

The size of the hole varies according to the seasons. Although there is evidence that the ozone layer over the North Pole is also affected, the destruction has not yet spread to the atmosphere above the middle and lower latitudes where most people, plants, and animals live.

## Ultraviolet radiation

Even a one percent increase in ultraviolet radiation can damage living things. If this happened, it is estimated that there would be 15,000 new cases of skin cancer in the United States, as well as an increase in the number of eye cataracts, which severely limit a person's sight. Plankton in the oceans supports marine life. It is very sensitive to ultraviolet radiation and, if it is damaged, could upset all life in the oceans. But this damage may be minor in comparison to the damage caused to DNA molecules. DNA carries the instructions to cells that determine the physical development of plants and animals. If the DNA molecules are damaged, then we can only guess at what could happen to living things.

The ozone layer also absorbs heat from the sun, warming the upper atmosphere. The less the amount of ozone, the less heat is absorbed. In turn this would lead to a change in the world's wind patterns that would cause changes to the climate and weather experienced at the surface. We have already seen that the heating of the earth through the ''greenhouse'' effect would also lead to changes in the climate and weather.

## Chlorofluorocarbons (CFCs)

The damage to the ozone layer is caused by a group of chemicals that are known as chlorofluorocarbons, or CFCs. They have many useful properties. For example CFCs do not affect

***The diagram** below **illustrates that CFCs are responsible for the damage to the ozone layer.***

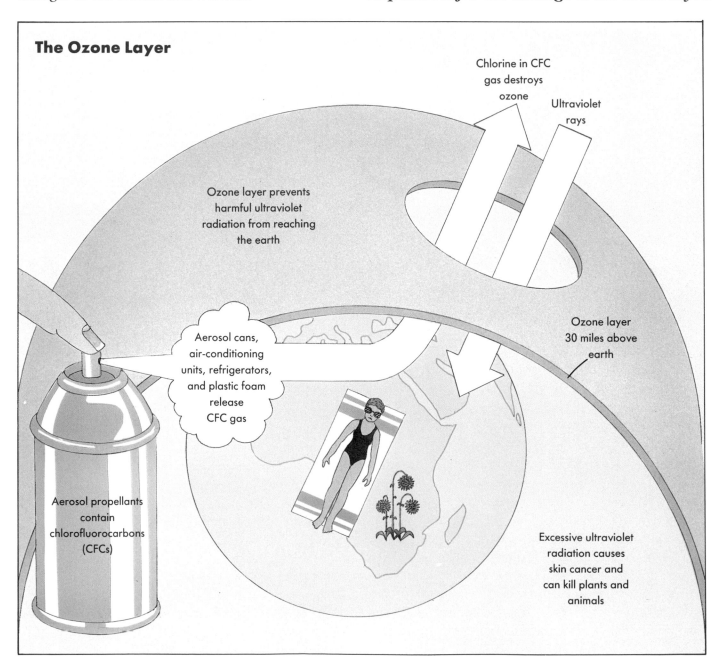

**The Ozone Layer**

Chlorine in CFC gas destroys ozone

Ultraviolet rays

Ozone layer prevents harmful ultraviolet radiation from reaching the earth

Aerosol cans, air-conditioning units, refrigerators, and plastic foam release CFC gas

Ozone layer 30 miles above earth

Aerosol propellants contain chlorofluorocarbons (CFCs)

Excessive ultraviolet radiation causes skin cancer and can kill plants and animals

Left *Today most households have a refrigerator and freezer. However, these contain a coolant that damages the ozone layer.*

Below *CFCs in aerosols have been banned in the United States since the 1970s. Now in many countries aerosol manufacturers are avoiding using CFCs.*

liquids. They do not change their color or smell, and they are not poisonous. They are perfect for using in aerosols to propel liquids through a nozzle in a fine spray and are used almost universally. Other uses of CFCs include cleaning microchips and circuit boards in the electronics industry, and making styrofoam cartons in which much fast food, such as hamburgers, is served.

One CFC called freon is particularly damaging to the ozone layer. It is used as the coolant in refrigerators. When the refrigerator is scrapped, the freon is released into the atmosphere.

## Action to solve the problem

Even if all CFCs were banned today, it would take fifty years for the ozone layer to return to normal. The seriousness of the problem can be judged by the speed at which action has been taken by the international community.

**Montreal Convention:** In 1987 the world's first treaty to limit CFCs was signed by twenty-seven nations, including the major industrial nations. They have agreed to reduce consumption of CFCs by 50 percent before 1990. However, this is not sufficient to solve the problem. Anything

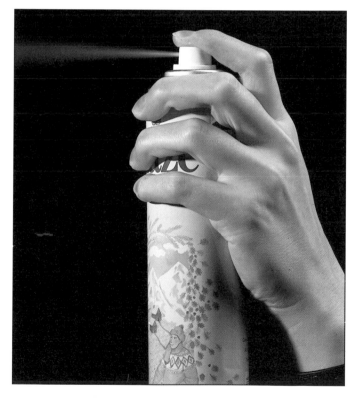

less than an 85 percent reduction is unlikely to prevent the problem from becoming worse. Many governments and industries have responded to pressure for stronger controls. The British government, for example, expected to reach the agreed reduction by 1989.

**Finding substitutes:** Before CFCs can be removed from the environment, scientists must find substitutes for them or alternative ways of doing the jobs CFCs do. There are substitutes that can be used in aerosols, and they have been used in the United States since the 1970s. Many industries are now using them and labeling those products as "ozone friendly." A firm in Florida claims to have developed an alternative for the electronics industry to use. The huge electronics company AT&T is using it and has already reduced its consumption of CFCs by 33 percent. More fast-food companies are now using packaging that can be made without CFCs.

**Research:** Now that the extent of the problem has been realized, it has prompted much more research into substitutes for CFCs and into monitoring the quality of the atmosphere in general.

## The outlook

The measures that are being taken to reduce the amount of CFCs in the atmosphere are very encouraging. They show what can be done and how quickly people can respond to environmental problems when consumers, governments, and industry work together to solve a problem. However, we must not think the problem is totally solved. We still have a long way to go before we can reduce the amount of CFCs by the required 85 percent. If we do achieve this reduction, it will indicate a positive change in our attitude toward the atmosphere.

*Right **The world's worst chemical accident occurred at Bhopal, India, in 1984. Following an explosion at the Union Carbide factory, a cloud of poisonous gas engulfed the surrounding area. Two thousand people died, along with much livestock. The survivors will suffer health problems for the rest of their lives.***

## Disposing of chemical waste

Chemicals are an important part of our lives. They are designed for many purposes, from killing pests in agriculture to cleaning microchips used in computers. Many of them are extremely dangerous and, once used, are difficult to dispose of. There are very strict controls on their use and disposal in most industrialized nations, but sometimes the controls are ignored or there is an accident. When this happens, dangerous fumes can be released into the atmosphere and breathed in by people.

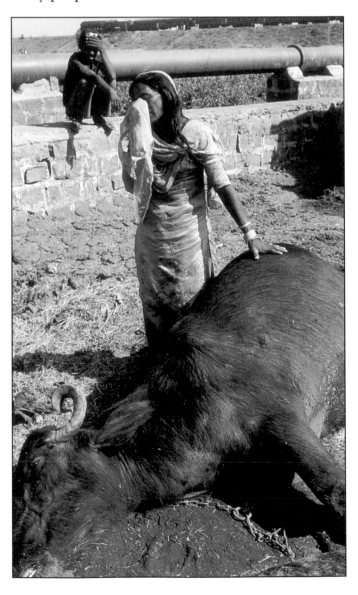

## Burning toxic waste

To make poisonous chemical wastes safe, they have to be burned at a very high temperature. One of the most dangerous groups of chemicals to living things are PCBs. They are so dangerous that it is illegal in Europe to find any new uses for them. However 220,000 tons will still have to be disposed of, probably by burning, when out-of-date electrical equipment in which they were used is scrapped. They must be burned at 3632°F for at least 22 seconds to be made safe. Failure to do this means that very poisonous fumes are released into the atmosphere. These include dioxin, which is the most poisonous chemical known.

The process of burning wastes is known as incineration. Because there is a danger of incinerators causing air pollution, they have been built on ships so that the burning can take place at sea—this is done mainly in Europe. Greenpeace is one environmental group that has campaigned against this, pointing to the piling up of dangerous wastes in the sea near the burning areas. One ship was releasing dioxin into the atmosphere.

*Dangerous chemicals can be disposed of safely if they are burned at very high temperatures. Special ships burn waste at sea, where controls are not strict. Whether burned on land or at sea, such chemicals still pollute the atmosphere.*

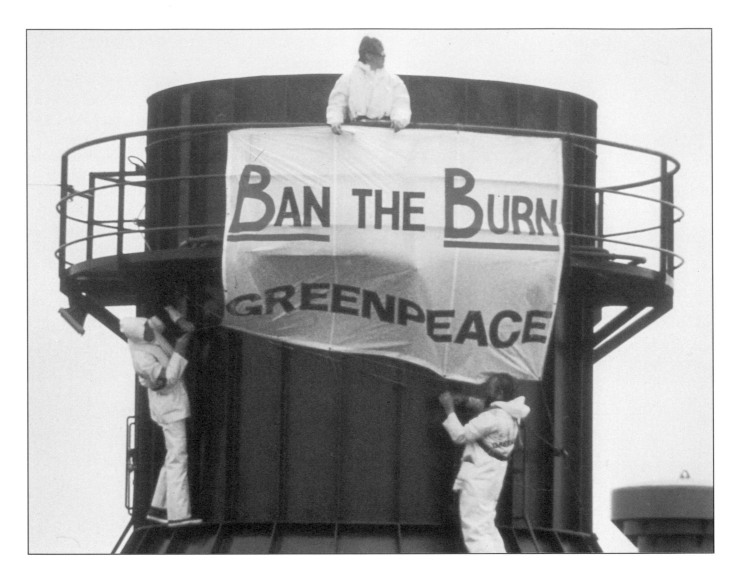

Pressure from environmental groups like Greenpeace and Friends of the Earth is one of the reasons why the London Dumping Convention agreed that burning wastes at sea should stop in 1994. A total of 65 nations have signed the agreement, and have also agreed not to export the waste to countries that have not signed the agreement. The Association of Maritime Incinerators, which has invested a lot of money in three special incineration ships, claims that such a ban is unnecessary. In 1992, it intends to produce scientific evidence that burning is safe and should be allowed to continue.

Although dangerous chemical wastes are also incinerated on land, most land-based incinerators

*To draw people's attention to the risks in burning dangerous waste at sea, Greenpeace stormed an incineration ship in the North Sea and tied this banner to the chimney. As a result of action like this, 65 nations have agreed to ban ocean incineration by 1994.*

burn domestic, hospital, and other wastes. Domestic waste presents a special problem, because it contains all kinds of garbage, some of which may release dangerous fumes into the atmosphere when burned. The same is true of neighborhood bonfires if they are also used to burn household waste.

**Right** *Roof beams are often treated with chemicals to prevent woodworm and dry rot. However, the chemical fumes can kill birds and bats that might be living there.*

**Below** *We can all help the environment by taking old paints, engine oil, and other chemicals to waste centers, where they can be disposed of safely. Never pour them down the sink or drain or on the ground.*

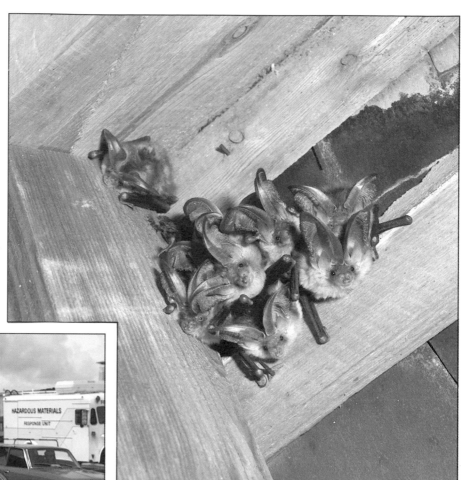

## Controlling pollution

Dangerous chemicals can escape into the atmosphere in many ways, so control is extremely difficult. Agricultural sprays can drift in the wind and damage hedges, trees, garden plants, and wildlife close by. Containers may leak, causing dangerous fumes to escape into the atmosphere. The fumes from wood preservatives used to protect timbers in the roof of a house may kill bats and birds, as well as the insects and fungi they are designed to kill.

Aware of the dangers, most countries have developed strict controls on the handling, use, and disposal of chemicals and chemical waste. However, enforcing the controls is a great problem, leaving ways for the careless and the unscrupulous to pollute the atmosphere.

37

There is probably no form of pollution that generates as much fear as radioactivity. Unlike many forms of air pollution, it cannot be seen or smelled. Its effects on living things are not always predictable and may take many years to develop.

We are already exposed to radioactivity, more commonly known as radiation, which comes from outer space or seeps out of the ground. Of all the radiation we receive, 87 percent is natural. The rest comes mainly from medical sources.

## Nuclear power

Nuclear power is a very controversial issue. A nuclear power station uses fuel that is highly radioactive and produces radioactive waste. Great care is taken to prevent any radioactivity from escaping into the atmosphere. Those who

***All forms of energy have advantages and disadvantages, as shown below.***

| Energy Sources | Cost | Benefit |
|---|---|---|
| Coal-oil-fired power station | Causes acid rain. Adds to global warming. Loss of land to mining. | Pollution can be controlled at a cost. Power station covers small land area. |
| Wind power | Can spoil landscape. Noisy. Large area of land needed. | No pollution. Fuel (wind) is free. |
| Hydroelectric power | Floods large areas of land, destroying the original habitat. | Creates new habitat for water creatures. No air pollution. |
| Wave power | Possible danger to shipping. Covers large area of sea. | Little building on land needed. No air pollution. |
| Nuclear power | Produces radioactive waste. Risk of harming environment if radioactivity leaks. | No air pollution unless radioactivity leaks. Power station covers small land area. |
| Solar energy | Requires large area of land for solar panels. | No air pollution. Renewable free energy source. |

favor nuclear power point out that it does not produce waste gases that contribute to the warming of the atmosphere or acid rain. It is "environmentally friendly." Those who oppose it point to the slight increase in background levels of radiation, the problem of disposing of radioactive waste, and the possibility of a terrible accident releasing radioactivity into the atmosphere. The explosion at Chernobyl provides evidence that nuclear power is unsafe.

## The impact of Chernobyl

The accident occurred at a nuclear power station in a sparsely populated area of the Soviet Union near Kiev in 1986. Only two people were killed by the explosion itself, but others died over the following weeks from radiation sickness because they were exposed to high levels of radioactivity. Thousands of other Soviet citizens will probably never know whether they have been affected.

The impact of the explosion was not restricted to the immediate area. A huge invisible cloud of radioactive gases escaped into the atmosphere and was blown by the wind over the surrounding countries. In Germany whole areas of food crops were contaminated and had to be destroyed. Animals grazing in areas where radioactive rain

*Chernobyl nuclear power station, Soviet Union, photographed after the 1986 accident which had such disastrous consequences.*

fell were found to be unsuitable for human consumption, and farmers had to rely on government support to stay in business. Even in 1988, some hill farmers in Great Britain are still unable to sell their sheep. It may be thirty years before the traces of radioactivity disappear.

## Nuclear power stations

Around the world there are about 350 nuclear reactors. When they are working normally, they are an expensive but clean way of producing electricity. However, if something goes wrong they have the potential to pollute the atmosphere in the most dangerous way. For many people the risks are too great to compensate for the benefits. In the United States, no new nuclear reactor has been commissioned since the serious accident at Three Mile Island in 1979. Sweden has voted to phase out nuclear power when its twelve stations have ended their useful life. Great Britain and France, on the other hand, are committed to expanding the number of nuclear power stations.

*In Britain, NIREX is responsible for finding a safe site for dumping nuclear waste, but few people want it near where they live.*

## The indoor atmosphere

Pollution is not just restricted to the air we breathe when we go outside. The atmosphere inside our homes may also be polluted. There are many causes of this pollution.

If central heating boilers, water heaters, open fires, and stoves using oil, solid fuel, or gas are badly maintained, they will use fuel inefficiently and cause more pollution. They can also give off dangerous fumes such as carbon monoxide.

In our attempts to conserve energy during winter, it is common to keep windows closed to seal up cracks that might cause a draft. There may be insufficient ventilation in a room and the air can become very stale. If someone is smoking, or there is an open fire, then the air can become very polluted.

Increasingly, smoking is becoming a controversial issue. Medical research has proven that cigarette smoke harms not only the smoker, but nonsmokers who inhale it.

Our kitchen cupboards, bathrooms, bedrooms, and garages are full of chemicals that we use without a second thought: bleaches, cleaning fluids, glues, polishes, and deodorants. Yet many of them pollute the atmosphere every time they are used. Just because a product smells nice does not necessarily mean it is good for you.

**Below right** *Smoking damages your health, but even nonsmokers are at risk if they spend much time in a smoky atmosphere. Now there are a growing number of areas for nonsmokers in public places.*

**Below** *Many household products can pollute the air indoors if not used properly. Always keep them well sealed and follow the instructions for their use and disposal.*

*Older jet aircraft can be very noisy. Jet engines used in newer passenger planes are designed to be much quieter.*

## Noise in the atmosphere

One form of atmospheric pollution is very different from those already mentioned. A noise that one person considers pleasant, such as loud music at a party, another living next door may find very annoying. Noise can be dangerous. The vibration from heavy traffic can damage buildings close by. If people are exposed to loud noises for long periods, this can permanently damage their hearing. For example, soldiers and people who often use guns may find a partial loss of hearing in the ear closest to the gun. Noise is becoming more frequently mentioned as an environmental issue as people are becoming much less tolerant of unacceptable noise levels.

In this book we have learned that the atmosphere protects the earth from meteorites and harmful radiation, that it regulates the temperature, and provides the oxygen and carbon dioxide necessary to support plant and animal life. We know it creates climate and weather patterns that farmers and others rely on. Left to itself, it would continue to provide these important services.

However, we have also learned that humans are using the atmosphere as a huge garbage dump for unwanted waste gases produced to support our way of life. These can be very unpleasant and even dangerous to breathe. More than that, they are changing the atmosphere and upsetting the delicate balance that has kept the world inhabitable for millions of years.

Some of the information you have read is undisputed scientific fact. For example, the amount of carbon dioxide in the atmosphere is increasing and the hole in the ozone layer does exist. These changes have been monitored and

*Los Angeles is famous for its haze caused by pollution. These smogs are becoming rarer as the authorities introduce measures to control air pollution, for example, strict checks on car exhaust emissions.*

recorded by instruments. Other information is not so straightforward. The majority of scientists agree that acid rain damages trees, but some say it still remains to be proved. The problem is that a tree may be weakened by acid rain but killed by insects. In cases like this, you will have to make up your own mind about who you think is right. You may realize you need more information before you can do this, in which case you can approach your teacher or your parents, visit the library, or write to one of the organizations listed at the back of this book.

There are many predictions about what will happen if we continue to pollute the atmosphere in the way we are. They are based on studies of what has happened in the past. These predictions are very important because the action we decide to take, or not to take, will be based on them.

We have also learned that we cannot take the environment for granted. All our activities change it, some for the better, some for the worse. Very often, we seem to forget that we are a part of nature and depend on it for everything. But there are limits to what it can provide, and when we try to push beyond these limits, we damage the environment.

It is now up to you to consider what you want to do. Are you happy to go along with the world the way it is, or do you want to change things? It is hoped that this book will have prompted you to think about one very important environmental issue and will help you decide what action you want to take.

*One theory predicts that if the rate of global warming continues, the climate of northern Europe will become similar to that in Mediterranean countries.*

# Glossary

**Acid**  A solution with a pH value of less than 7.0.

**Acid rain**  Rain, snow, or mist that has absorbed pollution in the atmosphere and become more acid.

**Aerosol can**  A container that holds liquids under pressure. The liquids are released in a fine spray through a nozzle.

**Atmosphere**  The gaseous layer that surrounds the earth and is held there by gravity.

**Cassava**  A tropical plant that has an edible rootstock.

**Catalytic converter**  A device attached to car exhausts to remove pollution.

**Chlorofluorocarbons (CFCs)**  The group of chemicals used in refrigerators and many aerosols that damages the ozone layer.

**Climate**  The long-term, prevailing weather conditions.

**Conservation**  Using resources in such a way that the environment is not damaged.

**Convention**  An agreement made by a group of countries to work toward a common goal.

**Dioxin**  A very poisonous industrial and agricultural chemical.

**DNA,**  or deoxyribonucleic acid. An acid found in the cells of organisms. DNA passes on hereditary characteristics from parents to offspring.

**Ecosystem**  A community of plants, animals, and other organisms and the environment in which they live and react to each other.

**Emissions**  Substances discharged into the air from chimneys and vehicle exhausts.

**Environment**  The surroundings in which all plants and animals live.

**Environmental pressure group**  Groups like Friends of the Earth and Greenpeace that campaign against polluting the environment.

**Fossil fuels**  Fuels obtained from organic substances, for example, coal, oil, and natural gas.

**Global warming**  The increase in the average temperature of the earth caused by the build-up of greenhouse gases in the atmosphere.

**Greenhouse gases**  The gases in the atmosphere that allow the heat of the sun to reach the earth, but slow down its escape.

**Hydrocarbons**  Organic material composed of carbon and hydrogen. It is the basis of fossil fuels.

**Nitrogen oxides (NOx)**  Gases formed mainly from nitrogen in the atmosphere when fuels are burned at high temperatures.

**Organism**  Any animal or plant that can maintain life by itself.

**Ozone ($O_3$)**  A form of oxygen that can damage plant growth and irritate the eyes and breathing system when it is concentrated near the surface of the earth.

**Ozone layer**  A narrow layer of ozone found in the upper atmosphere. It filters out the harmful ultraviolet radiation of the sun.

**pH**  The unit for measuring acidity.

**Photoelectric cell**  A device for converting light into electricity.

**Pollutants**  Substances that can damage the environment when released into it.

**Pollution**  The presence in the environment of harmful substances called pollutants.

**Predictions**  Forecasts of what is likely to occur in the future, based on scientific information.

**Radiation**  In this book, radiation is the word used to describe the movement of energy from one place to another through space or the air. Some forms are dangerous to humans.

**Radioactivity**  The radiation given off by certain materials.

**Sulfur dioxide ($SO_2$)**  A colorless gas with a strong odor formed primarily from burning fossil fuels.

**Toxic waste**  Waste material that is poisonous.

**Ultraviolet radiation**  Harmful, invisible light waves coming from the sun.

**United Nations**  The international organization that brings the world's countries together to discuss and attempt to solve world problems.

# Further Reading

## Books

Asimov, I. *How Did We Find Out About the Atmosphere?* (Walker, 1985).

Cochrane, J. *Air Ecology* (Watts, 1987).

Gay, K. *The Greenhouse Effect* (Watts, 1986).

Kiefer, I. *Posioned Land: The Problem of Hazardous Waste* (Macmillan, 1981).

Miller, C. and Berry, L. *Acid Rain* (Messner, 1987).

Schaefer, V. *A Field Guide to the Atmosphere* (Houghton Mifflin, Co., 1981).

## Map/chart

*Endangered Earth,* by the Editors of National Geographic Society (National Geographic Magazine, 1988).

## Pamphlet

*Industrial Leaks and Air Pollution: Causes, Cures and Health Concerns*, by Dr. Sukhraj S. Dhillon (Pamphlet Publications Publishing, 1988).

# Useful Addresses

**The Acid Rain Foundation**
1630 Blackhawk Hills
St. Paul, Minn. 55122

Aims to develop and raise public awareness of the issue and supplies educational resources.

**Acid Rain Information Clearing House**
Center for Environmental Information, Inc.
33 S. Washington Street
Rochester, N.Y. 14608

Provides general information about acid rain.

**Children of the Green Earth**
PO Box 95219
Seattle, Wash. 98145

Promotes and organizes children's tree planting projects and various educational activities. Publications.

**Conservation Foundation**
1250 24th Street N.W.
Washington, D.C. 20037

Promotes intelligent use of the earth's resources through research and communication. Publications, reports, and films.

**Friends of the Earth Foundation**
530 Seventh St., S.E.
Washington, D.C. 20003

Dedicated to education, research, litigation, and publishing for the preservation, restoration, and rational use of the earth's resources.

**Greenpeace U.S.A.**
1611 Connecticut Ave., N.W.
Washington, D.C. 20009

Initiates active measures to aid endangered species. Monitors conditions of environmental concerns including ocean dumping, acid rain, and test bannings on nuclear weapons.

**Izaak Walton League of America**
1401 Wilson Blvd., Level B
Arlington, Va. 22209

Works to educate the public on conserving, protecting, maintaining, and restoring the soil, forest, water, and other natural resources.

**Sierra Club**
730 Polk Street
San Francisco, Calif. 94109

Publishes a regular newsletter with details of environmental legislation in the United States.

**World Nature Association**
PO Box 673, Woodmoor Station
Silver Spring, Md. 20901

Naturalists—professional and amateur—interested in conservation and travel. Offers annual scholarship to an American educator in the natural sciences, grants for small research projects, conducts tours. Publications.

# Index

# Picture Acknowledgments

The publishers would like to thank the following for allowing their photographs to be reproduced in this book: Associated Press 28; Bruce Coleman Ltd 6 (Hans Reinhard), 10 below (Hans-Peter Merten), 11(B & C Alexander), 12 (D Houston), 19 (Cliff Hollenbeck), 20 above, 25 below (L C Marigo); Geoscience Features cover; Greenpeace 35, 36; Hutchison Library 14 above (P Edward Parker), 22 (R Ian Lloyd), 24 (Caran McCarthy), 31 (Bernard Regent); ICCE 29 (Mike Hoggett); Oxford Scientific Films 25 above (Sean Morris), 37 below (Doug Wechsler), 37 above (Michael Leach); Photri 7, 10 above; Rex Features Ltd 33 above, 34 (Haley), 39 (Bradwell); Paul Seheult 40; Frank Spooner 27 (Julian Parker); Topham Picture Library 13, 14 below, 15, 20 below, 26, 39 left, 41 below; ZEFA 4 (Mueller), 5 (C Voigt), 21, 30, 33 below, 41 above (G Kalt), 42 (J O'Rourke), 43 (K Kerth). The illustrations are by Marilyn Clay.